Praise to the Lord
of the Morning!

Praise to the Lord of the Morning!

Three Prayer Experiences

PATRICK MOONEY

With Photography by the Author

Ave Maria Press • Notre Dame, Indiana 46556

Library of Congress Catalog Card Number: 76-16673
International Standard Book Number: 0-87793-116-X (paper)
0-87793-115-1 (cloth)

Dedication

To my sister Susie
Whose love and support
Have given me
The courage to create.

PUBLISHER'S NOTE

Prayer and poetic sensitivity belong together. Reverence and worship are not expressed appropriately in business English.

But today it's rare to find poetic sensitivity which is accessible to—which can be enjoyed by—the ordinary reader.

Patrick Mooney has a rare combination of gifts. He is sensitive to the religious reality of modern life. But he also has a rare gift for expressing this religious sensitivity in words and photography which alert us to the echo of God in the persons and objects which have become too familiar to us.

Young people, too often alienated from religion and poverty, will feel comfortable with his insights; his language is linked to the lyrics of their song.

For all of us, however, he offers a rich experience of prayer pronounced in words and images of beauty.

John Reedy, C.S.C.

CONTENTS

INTRODUCTION

The meditations outlined in this book have been hammered out of the experiences of life. As prayer experiences they are meant as an invitation to put the pressures of the busy world aside. They ask that we surrender ourselves to the real God who can set us free.

Life is crammed with the presence of God. We have to dare to be different to hear his call and see his face. For those who have the courage to see, the whole world groans with the Incarnation:

Not a bird sings
But it echoes Christ's voice
And not a tree
Uplifts its branches
But in imitation of
His outstretched arms.

In order to see that all life is colored by Christ, we need the courage to see differently. A Christian is the person who sees the possibility of revelation where others see only stale routine. A Christian is the person who is child enough to wonder and question perpetually all over again. A Christian is the person who sees new possibilities and associations in everything.

Our times stereotype us and rob us of poetry and mystery. Technology has squeezed the juice out of our lives, so much so that we have become like shriveled-up orange peels. As technological people we are out of touch with God. We need desperately to discover contemplation all over again. We need urgently a new transcendent language capable of inspiring us back to our most original ground who is God.

The meditations in this book stem from a deep love for the color and glory of our world—the habitat from which the threads of human life are drawn and meshed. Each prayer derives its energy from the conviction that the good news of Jesus makes sense of the mystery and adds excitement and electricity to daily living. These prayers are meant to be meditated upon as an inter-connecting whole, although each may indeed be read as a separate entity.

Since this writer is convinced that the whole world is colored by the advent of Christ, there is, necessarily, a spiraling upward to Jesus as the Alpha and Omega of all human existence.

"A Song for God" is meant as the Alpha —the crib or creche of a sacred world into which Christ is placed. This meditation asks us to step aside from our busy world and rediscover wonder. It asks that we become children all over again and open ourselves to the beauty and great handiwork of God as he prevails in the midst of the little miracles of everyday life. Confronted by so much beauty and goodness we cannot but respond —we cannot but bow in adoration before the Creator of sunrise, food, beauty, human life and finally his most gracious gift—Jesus Christ. Jesus now becomes the mediator between earth and heaven. He is the outflow of God's unending goodness, the pivotal point of his love, the Connector between "A Song for God" and "The Living Bread."

Jesus came on earth to make us all brothers and sisters. He came to unite us into a community or a family. This is the essential meaning of Eucharist. We see in the latter part of "A Song for God" that Christ is spoken of as "Permanent Presence." Jesus Christ abides with us through a tremendous act of love—but he is present only to the extent that we work to find him. "The Living Bread" points out that we cannot receive Christ in the Eucharist in grand isolation. No, to receive the Eucharist is to live the Eucharist. To live the Eucharist is to identify with the Broken Christ, who walked on Calvary's hill. We cannot have Easter without Good Friday.

There is a definite connection then between Eucharist and the Paschal Mystery. Jesus said, "As the Father has sent me, so now I am sending you," and at another time he said, "By this shall all people know you, as my brothers and sisters, by your love for one another." So, what Christ has done for us, must now be done by us— we must become bread broken for others. This is no easy thing. It demands an affair of the heart. It means that we must reach out and "Touch and Heal" the lonely and the wounded and the oppressed as Jesus did. There is a definite connection, then, between "The Living Bread" and "Touch and Heal." "Touch and Heal" is the living out of "The Living Bread."

I

A Song for God

It is morning
And again the sun gives light to life

Splashing paints of glory
Upon the world

For eyes awake
To the giving hand of God

How good it is
To be alive
And breathe
The breaking breath of dawn

To hear the bird burst forth again
As trumpeter of the morn

Dark night
No longer her sovereignty plays
She has had her speech
Away
Away

God's People
Wake Up!
His hot breath
Is already upon the branch

His fiery eyes
In the furnaced sun

His benevolence in
The wheat head

He gives us bread
He gives us bread

Praise to the Lord
Of the morning
By his strong hand
We are fed
We are fed

Oh Giving Master
Oh Silent Presence
Behind the ebb and flow of life
Oh heartbeat of our sea

Take us by the hand again
Come and walk our crusted roads
And fill our bins with bread

Wake us up to life
Sacred soaked
In transfigured light
And give us dreams

Like the child
Who asks
Whose hand has painted
The wild field gold?

Ah but too soon we grow old
And our dreams are sold for harder things

How cold we are
Without your touch
Outcasts
In a wasted land
We rob your hand of gifts

Vulgar and smart
We lose your mystery
By computerizing
Your efficiency

And yet oh God
How great you are
You do not grow weary
Of our ways
Oh Patient Giver
Above us
Round us
Out us
In us
Despite our sin
Your love prevails

Despite the obstacles we put in your way
You strong stretch your hand
To furnace life

And faithful to your covenant call
Life obeys your law
Spring sprouts

And cells explode in mystery

Cows flood the earth
With milk butter

Meat lambs prepare our food
Among the hills

Groomed chicken
Graces the needy plate

Rivers tray trout

Fresh fruits
Fill the famished full

And the earth
Flesh flushed
Unwombs from her tomb of soil
The meticulous shapings of her
Crafted toil

God's People
Wake Up!
His benevolence is in the wheat head

He gives us bread
He gives us bread

Praise to the Lord
Of the morning
By His strong hand
We are fed
We are fed

Computer brains
Miss your presence Lord
For they do not hear you
Whisper in the rain

Nor have they ears to hear
Your heartbeat in the sea

Nor words enough
To sing you
Children's simple songs

Holy Artist
Give us eyes and ears again
To appreciate
Your brushed strokes of genius
In the air

May we know your hand
In the complex color
Of your provident care

House us from vulgarity
And let us stand in awe
At the small miracles
Hammered in your forge

Oh cause without cause
May we not deal deniance
And scream defiance
At your giving hand

When already
Your sacred generous light
Is amply painted upon the land

God's People
Wake Up!
He lives
And calls the earth to life

He abolishes boredom
By robbing drabness
Of its prey

A million throats of color
Chorus his presence
Each common day!

In vain
Do apothecaries
Seek to capture
The secret shadings of his hand

He speaks
And life bursts forth
From sod saddened by a winter's frost

And for the winter-weary
There are songs again upon the land

Oh denier of death
Oh mockery of monotony

Your giving hand is varied
You oil our clock

And life moves forth
To a fall full of veins

How astonishing are
The variegated stains
You paint upon the tree

Deep winter
Reflects the blueness of your eyes

Oh Artist Master
Help us arise

Give us surprise
Give us surprise

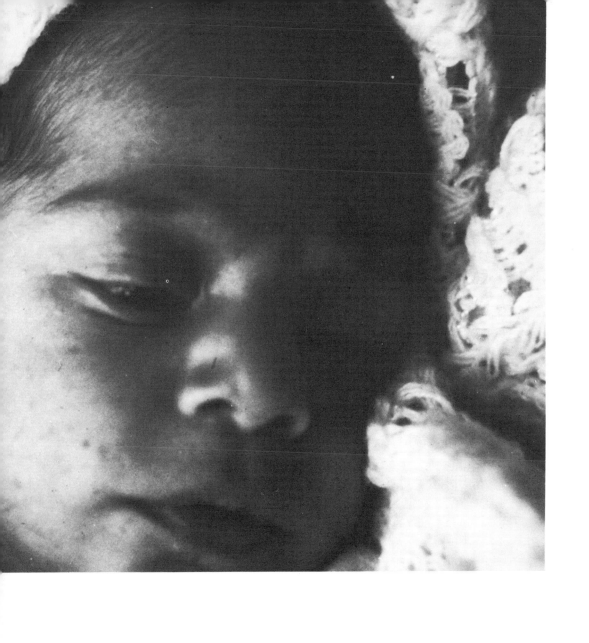

Men marvel at the works of man
And lavish praise

For the patented productions
Of his mind

But man is blind
To the presence behind
The staggering machinery of sacred life

Oh King of Architects
Oh Inventor of Inventors

You whose vision is the sea shore
And Einstein's by comparison
But a speck of sand

Fill us more
And take us by the hand

Make us revel in the miracles of your making

The hills and valleys
Of your perfect creation —

The human ear
So that we may hear
A mother call our name
In sacred love

A little hand
To grow in time
And touch
Another's heart
To lift and swell
The earth
With affirmation

Let the world
Lift its voice in praise
And thank you for a mouth to kiss

A little foot to walk

And
A tongue to taste the
Juice of life

Oh provider for survival
Engineer of every curve
Oh filter for our funnel

Wake us up to life
And give us sight

Be you the light
In our needy eyes
And fill us with your bread

Praise to the Lord
Of the morning
By his strong hand
We are fed
We are fed

It is morning
And again the sun gives light to life

Splashing paints of glory upon
The world

For eyes awake
To the giving hand of God

Oh Patient Giver
Oh basket that overflows
Brimming bringer
Circle of love

Ring that expands
To embrace the earth

How slow we are to accept the light
You give us dreams
And still we call the morning night

Love's atmosphere
Womb of life
You have heard the painful murmuring
On our shore
And in response
You reach again for gifts
And give us more
And give us more

Jesus your Son
Immortal Masterpiece
Heal-heart
Of human wound and want
Answer to our orphan call

Negator of absurd absence
Peak light of all

Has walked our rutted roads
And offered the world's hunger pangs
A loaf of bread

Avenger of the dark
In him the morning breaks
And drab dread
Scuttles to the grave
Before his feet

His laughter lives
In the loving eye

His healing for hunger
In the outstretched arm
Which helps the crippled walk

He is our Bread
Baked brown
And broken

Kneaded and gnarled
For men who care
To share and give

Oh heartbeat of yeast
Your dough prevails
And feeds us yet

Oh Permanent Presence
You do not forget our needs

Your benevolence is in the wheat head
You give us bread
You give us bread

Praise to the Lord
Of the morning
By his strong hand
We are fed
We are fed.

II

The Living Bread

PRAYER OF SURRENDER

Father
It is another incarnation day
Unique and different
Never born before

I, your priest
In the intense possession
Of this sacred moment
Arise
And greet the morning's expanding light

Spun as it is
Like a golden fabric
With the weaving thread
Of your vital presence

Already the bird has burst forth
From her brooding bracken
And with outstretched wings
She sings her praise
In trails across the waking sky

From suburban homes
Manicured like mannequins

From city buildings
Some thick with smut

Your human family
Some laughing
Some crying
In the new day's light
Make their way
And scurry like rabbits from burrows
In cars
Along the sterile convenient roads

Or sit impersonally in trains
Trapped and unfree
From the urgent demands
Of a consumer economy

For those who hurry past
Your window to life
And make new altars to a lesser god

For those who love your name
And sing your praise
Through their work

For the restless multitude
The oceans of shunting shifting travelers
Lost and alone
Searching for home

I, your priest
In this morning's sacred light
Embrace a human world
With my outstretched arms

And hank together
On this sacred table
As a bunch of grapes
All the heaving hopes and aspirations
Of your human family

In this morning's sacred light
I ask for Eucharist—courage—
May my process be
That of the gentle Jesus

Grapes crushed
To slake all human thirst

Bread broken
To feed the hungry full

Standing before you Father
In this time
Before the noonday sun
I humbly recognize
All human life
As a process into something greater

Flesh life
Is but a flicker
That waxes and wanes

And then
Like a plundered monastery
Devoid of the sounds
Of song and praise

It goes ghostly
Leaving the wind only
To conjure up the memory
Of a dead glory

Dissolution is an inbred fault
In the mechanics of human flesh
For bodies are born to be buried
And no man is complete unto himself

The full answer to life
Does not lie
In the synthetic greed and escapes
Commercialism offers

For all things pass away
Spring to winter
And earth to sky

Oh God
You are my consummation—
Through you
I shall not die
I hear you call . . .
Belief is all . . .

And so
Confronted by the conditions
And limitations of this human life
I, your priest, in this morning's sacred light
In the name of humankind
Reverently render respect
To your mighty name
As the beginning and end
Of all fleshly existence

You are the transcendent magnet
Ever pulling us up and on
Give us courage then
Help us fly
And do not let us die upon the vine

With outstretched arms
I raise my spirit as a humble suppliant
And make my Eucharist to your incomparable
    presence

As arbiter
Between the forces of doubt and faith
Love and hate
I, your priest
Stand on this mountaintop
And make this morning's altar
The table upon which
I place all the confused letters of men

Who shout their curses
At your face
For life's cruelties and uncertainties

There is so much I cannot answer

I stand before your holy presence
In my half-baked sight
And ask for light to carry on

Ultimately I know
The only possible answer
Is the answer
That there shall be no answer
Until the day
Of one's spent harvest has come in

Time is relative
And patience divine

Eventually, you, the eternal spring
The magnetizing energy of our being
The outer limit of our touch
Will set the crooked ways straight
And bring us home
This I believe

There is cruelty—yes
In a world
Where men hate
Where wars whip and wound
Where children die . . .
I do not know why

But in the meantime
I take heart in you
The eternal source of life
And thank you
For your overflowing spring of fresh water
Through Jesus your Son
Who walked our dusty roads
And pierced the void of our dark

Who offered us drink
To slake our everlasting thirst

Who offered us Bread
To quench the fear of our mortal hunger

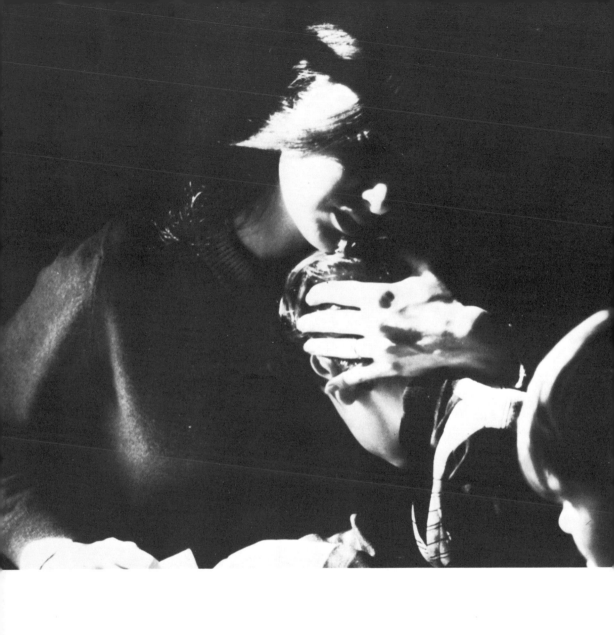

I thank you
For the sustenance of sacred food
For a world where so much goes right
If we will but count it
Where beauty coats the valley
And the hills play host
To the deer's wild run

I thank you
For all that is holy through
Mothers who bind and heal our wounds

Through fathers who plow our fields
And work our world
To keep us clothed and fed

And I take heart
In your presence
Through the joy of children
Who play their games
And dance their little lives
Upon the hill

Christ, Oh Christ have mercy
The world groans with your presence
But so often
I, your priest
Have compartmentalized my life
And put you in a neat box

Adding you
As just another curiosity
To be gathered in
And placed among my collection of trivia
Far from the center of my being
And the energizing source of my life

Relegating your importancy
To the back bench of my life
Ashamed of my Christian call to witness

My silent voice
Has screamed approval
To the throated mob
Who wants to drown your word

Lord
Oh Lord have mercy

And so often in pride
For not allowing God to be God
And I
His dependent child

Christ
Oh Christ have mercy
Forgive me Jesus
Empty me and make me over
Make me as your own

And so
In the bravery of this moment
On this sacred morning
At this holy altar
I, your priest
Once again, in the midst of all my uncertainties
And consumed with the search of human confusion

Stand as a child
Naked and vulnerable
Before your infinite majesty

Once again
I reach out
And ask that the cleansing water of your love
Will purify me
Of all that is insincere, selfish and unsacred
And again
That I shall learn where home is
And shall stand before you
Spotless and joyous
As a young child
Who has found laughter
And freedom
Upon the hill

Be more to me
The staff and strength of my crutch
For I am lame Lord
And want to learn
How to walk

PRAYER OF OFFERING

This morning
Your holy people
Across the world
Whether in cathedral or hut
Monastery or hall

Bring you
The gifts of their fields
And the toil of their hands
As a sacrificial offering

Take them Father
And through your mystic presence
Fuse the gifts of the few

To the countless millions absent
Who perhaps confusedly wind their way
Through the labyrinths of your world
With no thought of your hand
On this holy day

Make us all one
As the shoot upon the stem
And the grape upon the vine

May we become crushed
As many grapes
To become one cup of wine
For Eucharist means union
And so, this morning
I, your priest
In memory of Jesus
The community builder

Place in this cup
All the hopes and aspirations
Of your human family

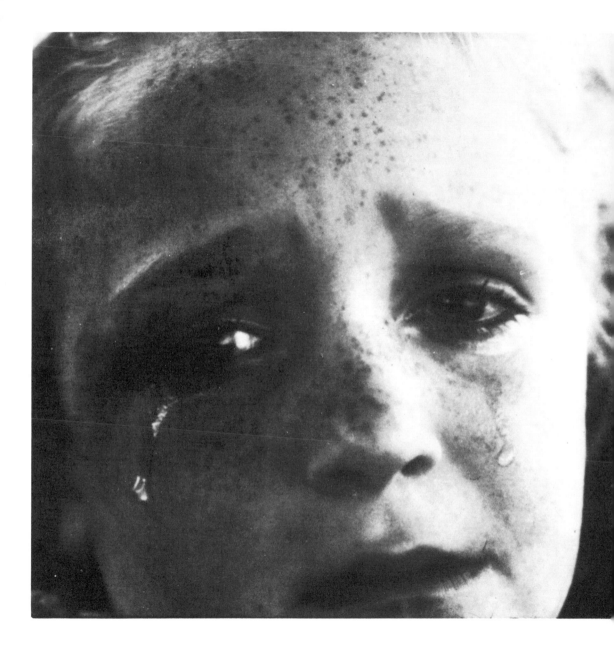

Inescapably on this morning of waking light
Life explodes
With its customary share
Of increase and loss

Through life's uncompromising regularity
Some will laugh
And some will cry this day

For all who cry I pray
And most especially
My offering shall be
For little Michael McTique
Whom the doctors said
Would not hear or see
Good boy Michael
You have come a long way
And fooled us all
For you I pray

That you too shall play
Your little games
Upon the hill

Oh Christ
You have shown the healing way
Through selfless love
Help us climb the hill with you
This sacred day. For Michael I pray.

June penned her words in desperation
And shoved a crumpled note into my hand.
I feel inadequate
And horribly pained
But I must be present to her needs

Oh Christ
You have shown the healing way
Through selfless love
Help us climb the hill with you
This sacred day. For June I pray.

Sister Mary Denis
Has lost the use of her legs
She who gladly drained her life for others
Now she only looks out
Where once she walked

She who loves so much
The wild flowers of the field
And the small birds of the air
I want to cry

But she only laughs and shows me courage
True freedom lies with those so close to God

And so
I wish her songs upon her windowsill
And the blowing air of spring
Through her little room

Oh Christ
You have shown the healing way
Through selfless love
Take us by the hand
Open our minds
And teach us how to share the need of a friend

Open our hearts
So that we may learn how to live again
Help us climb the hill with you
This sacred day. For Sister Mary Denis I pray.

Oh Holy One of Nazareth
God's Son
Your promises bring my cold life spring
Like shoot from stem
I turn my face to a warmer sun
And burst into the newness of a greater life
You are the leaves upon my tree

With all the exciting intensity
Of lovers who run
To pluck and place
Some urgent kisses
Upon each other's quivering lips
You excite me

In you
My stream of life
Finds its final destiny
You are my sea

You gave us bread
To break our bread with one another
For that is what you said
"By this shall all men know you as my brothers
By your love for one another."

PRAYER OF CONSECRATION

And so it was
On that holy night
Before you died

Despite the intensity of your human terror
While men like devouring wolves
Planned your torture
Outside that supper room door

Still you
The peaceful courageous man of Nazareth
Calm, though frightened
Thought of your friends
And called them to a holy meal

Baked bread
Became your broken Body
When you said

"This is my Body Broken
Take it and eat it
Whenever you do this
You will do it in memory of me"

Oh sensitive visionary
Oh Christ of love and life
Too well you knew
The pain of separation
Your road to life is a lonely one

Your friends are gathered
For your meal of departure
Your absence will be a severing blow
To all their plans and dreams
Why must it end like this
In such terrible confusion

Ah but gentle Jesus
Your life is a paradox
You know too well the human heart
You teach your friends
One only finds by losing
One only receives by giving away
Blood spilled
Spells life as well as death

And so
You took the cup of wine
And said

"This is my blood poured out for you
Whenever you do this
You will do it
In memory of me"

Oh Christ of Nazareth
Your Eucharist is not an easy thing
For it is linked to death for the sake of life

We your human family
All too weak, selfish and cowardly
So often fail and fall
We renege on your call
To become bread broken
For the sake of life

In memory of you
We are afraid to become
Community builders
To threaten the world with your love

Forgive us Jesus
All too clearly
Now I see
The relationship between this holy meal and
    Calvary

They come in droves
The lonely maimed
The imprisoned and the tortured
The starving hordes
The lonely souls
The repressed and the depressed
From penned houses
Of hell and hate

I hear their howls
As they reach and screech
For the solace of your love

I become afraid and frightened
To live your call

To become bread broken
To feed the hungry
And grapes crushed
To slake the screech of human thirst

Calvary is a daily occurrence
Both for the victim and the murderer
And so often Jesus
In recent times
My selfishness
Has banged the hammer harder
On your hands
And I have made you hang again
By seeking self-sought loves
Instead of you
My unselfish friend

But strengthened by your love
I, your priest
Rededicate myself to your call
And in this morning's sacred light
Embrace the restless multitudes
In my outstretched arms
The oceans of shunting shifting travelers
Lost and alone
Searching for home

And hank together
On this sacred altar
As a bunch of grapes
All the heaving hopes
And aspirations of your human family

With your love
I am warm
And strong enough
To conquer any storm

My altar shall not be
A haven of isolation
But one lived out
In the arena of a world
That is starving for
All the innocence and laughter
Of your gentle touch

I know too well
That your Eucharist Christ
Cannot be confined
To the riskless surrounding of this table

But must be a lived experience
Hammered out on the anvil
Of a confused world
In the midst of all human hate and darkness

What you have done for us
Must now be done by us
For you have said
"As the Father has sent me
So now I am sending you"

Like shoot from stem
With our roots in you
We are comforted by your promise

Yet challenged by your call
To leave the safety of the sanctuary
And sow your seed of love

Compelled to see you
In our shackled brothers
The men and women
Who walk life's dusty roads
With no place to go
And no hand to make their burden light

Filled with your Father's presence
You went forth
And were strong enough
To become our Savior
On Calvary's hill

For once so long ago
On that thunder day
When brute men
Clubbed and clawed
Your perfect body
Into a blood-soaked shroud
You cried aloud
Forgiveness for their deed
And so taught our world
That love is not madness
But a need and a seed

May I, your priest
Of consecration
In memory of your name

May we, your priests of dedication
Suffused with the healing power of your presence
Among us

Now go forth
To plow the fallow field
And become your Eucharist

Wheat heads broken to
Feed the famished
Grapes crushed
To slake all human thirst

And so
This morning Jesus
As the world awakens
To new energies and potentialities
I, your priest
Called to a covenant response
Vest myself more
In the cloak of your love

Help me feel more
The pulse of your pain
That very life-giving process
From Calvary's hill

Through which
All newness, all relationships
All union, all brotherhood is born
Christ make us one

How paradoxical
That we, the living children
Of human mothers
Should enter this world
Through their labor pains

Their moans and groans
For our deliverance

And how soon
That pain converts to joy
When mothers see
Their children grow
And play their little games
Upon the hill

Ah all too clearly Christ
Now I see
The connection between
The joy of your Eucharist
And the pain price you paid
On Calvary

Once in response
Having paid the price
For the sake of life
And learned to climb
Calvary's hill with you

Soon our pain converts to joy
Morning breaks into an Easter sky
We are not orphans
Nor abandoned to die
The cross disappears
And allays all fears
For love is immortal
And life is eternal
Upon that hill

We no longer wind
As restless multitudes
Or oceans of shifting shunting travelers
Lost and alone
In you oh Christ
The human family
Finds its home

Peace comes
With all sharing
And cure comes
With caring
And home is spelled
With the "h" from heal
Instead of hate

And so
I come to you Christ
With all the excited
Intensity and expectancy
Of lovers who run
To pluck and place
Some urgent kisses
Upon each other's quivering lips

You excite me
In you oh Christ
Our stream of life
Finds its final destiny
You are our sea
For by your wounds
We are all set free

Already the bird has burst forth
From her brooding bracken
And with outstretched wings
She sings her praise
In trails across
The waking sky

We too go forth
To celebrate
With exultation
The glories of your creation
On this holy incarnation day

Replenished with your love
May we forge new dreams
For a better world
And may your holy peace be in our hearts
And your love like a mantle
Cloaked around our being

And so we go
Our future is in your hand
We walk with you
Belief is all
And home is our hope.
Thank you Father. Amen.

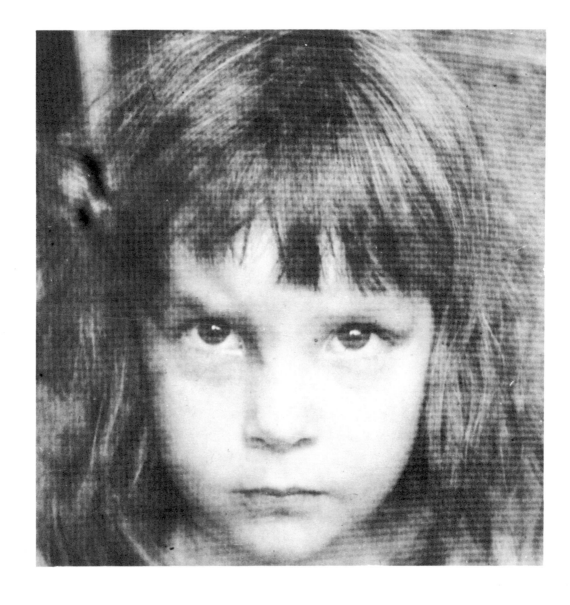

III

Touch and Heal

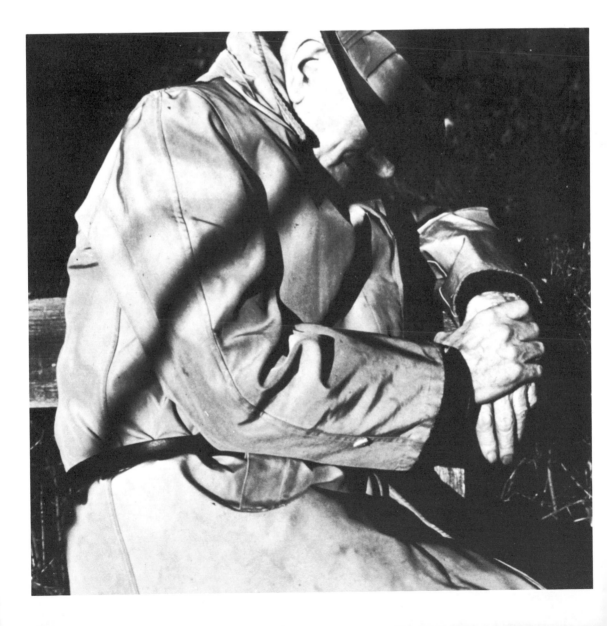

Streams come and streams go
But in the rush
Have we heard
The whisper of his call?

Whenever you do it to one of these
The least of my brothers
You do it to me

Africa . . . so far away
So far . . . so far we say
Distance makes us indifferent—
Our great cop-out
On Christian commitment

I am thirsty . . .
Whenever you give a drink
To one of these
The least of my sisters
You give it to me

India . . .
So far away
So far . . . so far we say
Distance makes us indifferent—
Our great cop-out on Christian commitment

We spend twenty billion dollars a year
On dog and cat food

India is not so far away . . .
Her starving hordes
Haunt the shelves
Of our immoral ways

The money we spend on a long-playing record
Could feed a starving Indian family
For a week

Out there beyond the horizoned hill
Of our pampered raveled sight
The ravaged poor
Interned in savage hovels
Crouch
And scratch
The bony soil
In search of hope

Condemned as common criminals
The poor are fenced out
By the feigned security of our minds
We do not allow
The deep-down mud from their lives
To spatter the windows
Of our manicured ways

But wounds need bandages
And not indifference
Or else they fester
And breed a plague
More plaguing yet

As keepers of the purse
The pampered gloat
And play Pharaoh or Messiah
On consecutive days
But justice is a Christ
Of more consistent ways
Relentlessly, like a revolution
She insists
There is no peace
While some starve
And others feast

Men cannot expect
Untroubled days
And easy nights
While some eat chaff
And others wheat

Sociologists tell us
The only thing
The rich have going for them
Is the patience of the poor

But how long Oh Christ
How long?

No person should say
"Oh what the hell's the use
No matter what I do
It makes no difference
In the conflict of nations"

The greatest war of all
Is won or lost
On the battlefield
Of a man's own soul

And so
Distance should not determine indifference
For there are many Africas
And many Indias
To be battled for within oneself or
On the doorstep of our own backyard

One person can make a difference
Just as one man did once save the world
By stripping himself
And dying naked upon a tree

Mightier
And more monied men than he
Have all gone their way unremembered
But the shredded bones of his broken Body—
The wasted madness of his love
Still stand clear
To haunt and challenge us

They say what words cannot dare say:
"The Body Broken
Is the process of resurrection
And love wasted
Is life gained"

Oh people of the Lord
Look up!
Emmanuel is on the doorstep of our world

He lives among us
In the tattered shreds of humanity
And his cradle is the cup
In our caring hand

Africa and India
Are not so far away
That we use distance
As a cop-out on commitment

The glaring eyes of the hungry
Peep out from the savage packages
Of our pampered ways

It's a fierce scandal
To the Christ of Life
When a pound of dog flesh
Sells for more
On the market of our human heart
Than a fellow human being
With all his scabs and sores

Oh yes
There are many Africas
And there are many Indias

In the value choices
We make for life
Each common day

Shall we go on hoarding
And bulging our closets
With nonessentials? If so
Nature will have the final say

There is another way
And another cup
That must be filled
For thirst is as much a thing of the soul
As it is of the stomach—The bread of one's body
Is the process of life

For he has said
Whenever you give a drink
To one of these
The least of my brothers
You give it to me

Africa and India
Are not so far away
They are within us
In the value choices
We make for life each common day

So light the candle of your heart
And bring brightness to the world
In your own small way

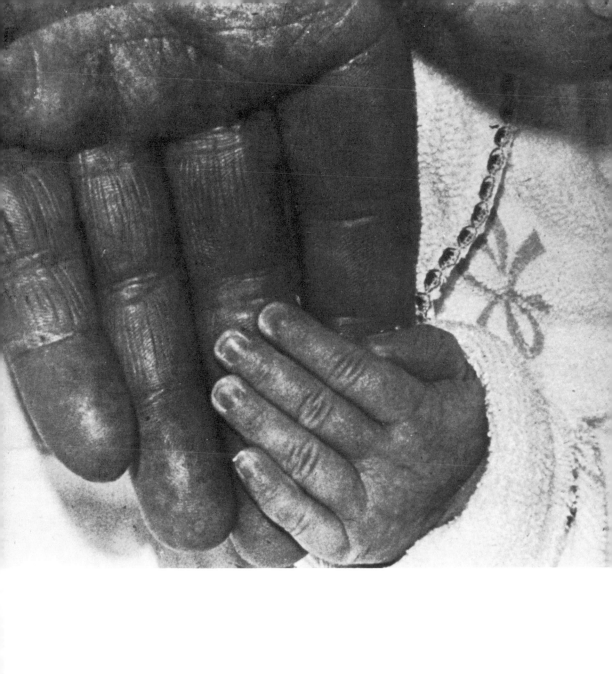

The problems of the earth
May be too awesome
For our own small shoulders—
But let's hone them down to our own size
For reconciliation begins
With the touch
Of our own little hand

The harmony of the world
Begins at home
In the choices we make to touch and heal

Global
Brotherhood has its birth
Around the small environment
Of our kitchen tables

Old Mary
Has been shoved into a death house
Because there's no room for her
In our youth-crazed culture

How convenient to have
Such an easy solution to the problems of life!

Put them in boxes and cover them
Up in attractive wrappings

Mary's loneliness . . .
Her terrible loneliness
Cries out to our indifference
In a smothered stillness

She is our India
Not so far away
She calls, but we do not hear—
She might as well be in India or Africa or
Somewhere far away

Old John lives on Skid Row
I asked him what he did to pass his day

And he snarled back
"Oh what the hell do you think I do
But try to exist
Like everyone else"

And then he stood again
A shivering sack of humanity
Shattered and shackled
By the pharisaical eye
Of a self-righteous society

And I knew at once
What I had meant to him
Like everyone else
I was part of the earth's crime
Who made part of the earth's life
No one to everyone and
Only someone to himself

He is our Africa
Not so far away
An opportunity among
Millions of others
For healing reconciliation in our day

Indifference is the greatest indictment
Of the Christian world
And Christ the Great Failure
Loves us more for our efforts
Than our successes

Bridges depend upon the support of pebbles
And the world is saved
To the extent that we give as Christed individuals

Africa and India surround us daily
They are the familiar countries of the heart
And have their frontiers
In the human soul

Any person at all
Is the nucleus of that love circle
Which can bring reconciliation to the world

Any person at all
May lend a hand
As a link of concern
In that chain of unity
Which heals the earth

Each person in love is a blazing torch of hope
     for the earth
For the earth is potentially
The same family
As any human home.

Streams come
And streams go
But in the rush
Have we heard
The whisper of his call?